HOW TO BE A
HUGE
SUCCESS

UNBEATABLE advice from life's big WINNERS

Managing Editor: Simon Melhuish
Series Editor: Lee Linford
Design: Alan Shiner

Designed and compiled by
Mad Moose Press
for
Lagoon Books
PO Box 311, KT2 5QW, UK
PO Box 990676, Boston, MA 02199, USA

ISBN: 1-904139-26-4

www.madmoosepress.com
www.lagoongames.com

Printed in Hong Kong

HOW TO BE A
HUGE
SUCCESS

UNBEATABLE advice from life's big **WINNERS**

According to Andy Warhol, everybody will experience at least 15 minutes of fame. There are a select few, however, who manage a little longer; occasionally some who seem destined to make an indelible mark in the history books. So what exactly does it take to become a legend?

Whether the road to success is down to luck, destiny, being in the right place at the right time or just sheer hard work, blood, sweat and tears, it's worth remembering that practically every somebody was once a nobody.

Sylvester Stallone ushered cinema audiences to their seats before he ended up with starring roles in the movies themselves. He was in good company; Al Pacino and Elvis did the same before fame came knocking at their doors. Not quite the glamour they found later in life but surely preferable to Sean Connery's job polishing coffins or Madonna's stint selling doughnuts.

For those wondering what it takes to make the transition from coffin polisher to movie megastar or how to become a guiding force over the course of world politics, then read on.

With quotes, quips and tips from a plethora of pop idols, movie stars, sporting celebrities, writers, artists, scientists, philosophers, politicians, world leaders and business tycoons, you'll find some truly inspirational and winning words throughout this book.

In the struggle between the stone and the water, in time, the water wins.

Chinese Proverb

A man is not finished when he's defeated; he's finished when he quits.

Richard Nixon

Only a man who knows what it is like to be defeated can reach down to the bottom of his soul and come up with the extra ounce of power it takes to win when the match is even.

Muhammad Ali

I've been lucky before. I'll be lucky again.

Bette Davis

I didn't come into politics to change the Labour Party. I came into politics to change the country.

Tony Blair

There's a wink behind everything I do.

Madonna

It may be hard for an egg to turn into a bird: it would be a jolly sight harder for it to learn to fly while remaining an egg. We are like eggs at present. And you cannot go on indefinitely being just an ordinary, decent egg. We must be hatched or go bad.

C. S. Lewis

Fame is a bitch, man.

Brad Pitt

Life's battles don't always go to the stronger or faster man. But sooner or later the man who wins, is the man who thinks he can.

Vince Lombardi

Show me a good loser and I will show you a loser.

Paul Newman

The important thing is not to stop questioning. Curiosity has its own reason for existing.

Albert Einstein

I don't continually question my reason to live. It's just a state of being. The real question is what you're doing with the living you're doing, and what you want to do with that living.

Mick Jagger

If you can dream it, you can do it. Always remember that this whole thing was started with a dream and a mouse.

Walt Disney

It has never been my objective to record my dreams, just the determination to realize them.

Man Ray

Never tell people how to do things. Tell them what to do and they will surprise you with their ingenuity.

General George Patton

If I have seen further than others, it is by standing on the shoulders of giants.

Sir Isaac Newton

Dream as if you'll live forever; live as if you'll die tomorrow.

James Dean

Sex appeal is 50% what you've got and 50% what people think you've got.

Sophia Loren

Even I don't wake up looking like Cindy Crawford.

Cindy Crawford

Victory at all costs, victory in spite of all terror, victory however long and hard the road may be; for without victory there is no survival.

Sir Winston Churchill

Being number two sucks.

Andre Agassi

If you can't make it good, at least make it look good.

Bill Gates

The whole thing is to keep working and pretty soon they'll think you're good.

Jack Nicholson

Genius is one percent inspiration, ninety-nine percent perspiration.

Thomas Edison

I don't know if I even have an aura, man. I just try to win.

Tiger Woods

Look at a day when you are supremely satisfied at the end. It's not a day when you lounge around doing nothing. It's when you've had everything to do and you've done it.

Margaret Thatcher

In the end, everything is a gag.

Charlie Chaplin

Timing is the essence of life.

Bob Hope

Eighty percent of success is showing up.

Woody Allen

Strength does not come from winning. Your struggles develop your strengths. When you go through hardships and decide not to surrender, that is strength.

Arnold Schwarzenegger

The only thing we have to fear is fear itself.

Franklin D. Roosevelt

The secret of getting ahead is getting started.

Agatha Christie

It takes as much energy to wish as it does to plan.

Eleanor Roosevelt

Lord, grant that I may always desire more than I can accomplish.

Michelangelo

If a man is called to be a streetsweeper, he should sweep streets even as Michelangelo painted, or Beethoven played music, or Shakespeare wrote poetry.
He should sweep streets so well that all the hosts of heaven and earth will pause to say, here lived a great streetsweeper who did his job well.

Martin Luther King Jr

A rough road leads to the stars.

NASA

What counts is not necessarily the size of the dog in the fight - it's the size of the fight in the dog.

Dwight B. Eisenhower

My dad always used to tell me that if they challenge you to an after-school fight, tell them you won't wait - you can kick their ass right now.

Cameron Diaz

Hidden talent counts for nothing.

Nero

To talk well and eloquently is a very great art, but an equally great one is to know the right moment to stop.

Wolfgang Amadeus Mozart

What's money? A man is a success if he gets up in the morning and goes to bed at night and in between does what he wants to do.

Bob Dylan

A man who dares to waste one hour of time has not discovered the value of life.

Charles Darwin

If you want to make peace with your enemy, you have to work with your enemy. Then he becomes your partner.

Nelson Mandela

A leader is a dealer in hope.

Napolean Bonaparte

Even if you're on the right track, you'll get run over if you just sit there.

Will Rogers

Without deviation, progress is not possible.

Frank Zappa

The ultimate measure of a man is not where he stands in moments of comfort, but where he stands at times of challenge and controversy.

Martin Luther King Jr

Education is an admirable thing, but it is well to remember from time to time that nothing that is worth knowing can be taught.

Oscar Wilde

I taught them everything they know, but not everything I know.

James Brown

Winning isn't everything. Wanting to is.

Catfish Hunter

Next to knowing when to seize an opportunity, the most important thing in life is to know when to forgo an advantage.

Benjamin Disraeli

A man of genius makes no mistakes. His errors are volitional and are the portals of discovery.

James Joyce

Have no fear of perfection - you'll never reach it.

Salvador Dali

If I get big laughs, I'm a comedian. If I get little laughs, I'm a humourist. If I get no laughs, I'm a singer.

George Burns

In order to be irreplaceable, one must always be different.

Coco Chanel

I'm always thinking about creating. My future starts when I wake up every morning. Every day I find something creative to do with my life.

Miles Davis

The act of creating is as integral a part of life as going to the lavatory.

David Bowie

Failure has no friends.

John F. Kennedy

Man is free.
The coward
makes himself
cowardly.
The hero makes
himself heroic.

Jean-Paul Sartre

I take rejection as someone blowing a bugle in my ear to wake me up and get me going, rather than a retreat.

Sylvester Stallone

Sometimes the road less traveled is less traveled for a reason.

Jerry Seinfeld

Don't compromise yourself. You are all you've got.

Janis Joplin

Nothing is so exhausting as indecision, and nothing is so futile.

Bertrand Russell

Twenty years from now you will be more disappointed by the things that you didn t do than by the ones you did do. So throw off the bowlines, sail away from the safe harbor. Catch the trade wind in your sails. Explore. Dream. Discover.

Mark Twain

Imagination is more important than knowledge.

Albert Einstein

Free your mind and your ass will follow.

George Clinton

Great things are not accomplished by those who yield to trends and fads and popular opinion.

Jack Kerouac

Leadership is a potent combination of strategy and character. But if you must be without one, be without the strategy.

Norman Schwarzkopf

Give me a firm place to stand and I will move the earth.

Archimedes

Give me six hours to chop down a tree and I will spend the first four sharpening the axe.

Abraham Lincoln

I never said "Well, I don't have this and I don't have that." I said, "I don't have this yet, but I'm going to get it."

Tina Turner

The most difficult thing is the decision to act, the rest is merely tenacity. The fears are paper tigers. You can do anything you decide to do. You can act to change and control your life; and the procedure, the process is its own reward.

Amelia Earhart

If one takes care of the means, the end will take care of itself.

Mahatma Gandhi

Luck is where opportunity meets preparation.

Denzel Washington

There is one thing stronger than all the armies in the world: and that is an idea whose time has come.

Victor Hugo

There is always some kid who may be seeing me for the first or last time. I owe him my best.

Joe DiMaggio

A career is born in public, talent in private.

Marilyn Monroe

Nobody ever drowned in his own sweat.

Ann Landers

Be like a duck. Calm on the surface, but always paddling like the dickens underneath.

Michael Caine

Don't pay any attention to what they write about you. Just measure it in inches.

Andy Warhol

The less you know, the more you believe.

Bono

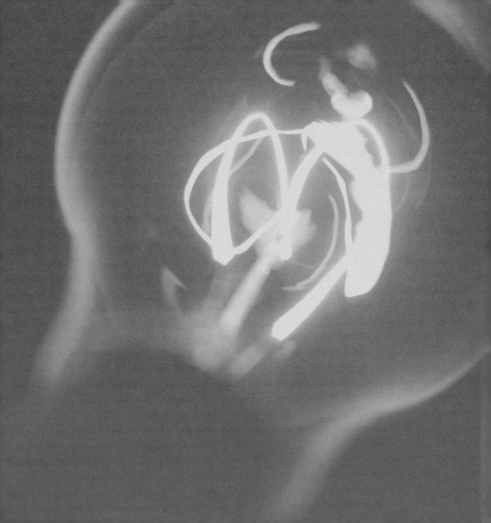

Genius is a little boy chasing a butterfly up a mountain.

John Steinbeck

You'll have time to rest when you're dead.

Robert De Niro

It ain't over till it's over.

Yogi Berra

for even more insightful

advice, check out

'How to be Filthy Rich',

also available from

Mad Moose Press.